D1050419

BECOMING A
CREATIVE
GENIUS
{again}

CARL NORDGREN

Torchflame Books
An imprint of Light Messages

Becoming a Creative Genius {again}
Carl Nordgren
www.creativepopulist.com
carl@creativepopulist.com

Published 2016, by Torchflame Books
    an Imprint of Light Messages
www.lightmessages.com
Durham, NC 27713 USA
SAN: 920-9298

Paperback ISBN: 978-1-61153-216-6
Ebook ISBN: 978-1-61153-217-3

Cover design and layout by Kevin Qian
www.qbranding.com
panasonicyouth0@gmail.com

PRAISE FOR
BECOMING A CREATIVE GENIUS (again}

'Becoming a Creative Genius {again}' is a great guide for all of us to reclaim the creativity that we all had as kids before conformity, peer pressure, and following too many well-worn paths stripped it all away from us. It's still there though, and this book helps you rediscover the joy of being creative and leveraging it to bring you happiness and success. George L. Grody - Visiting Professor Duke University, Procter & Gamble (retired)

'Becoming a Creative Genius {again}' is important. It reminds us of the inherent ability each of us had as children to imagine, play and create. More importantly, it provides numerous lessons and exercises to help us rediscover and rekindle those likely now underutilized characteristics. In today's dynamic world, our creativity is critical to thriving and contributing. Read this book and rediscover your creative genius {again}. Tom Triumph, CEO of Orbital Environments, whose clients include SpaceX, Virgin Galactic, and NASA

Carl Nordgren, our dad, has been one of our greatest teachers. Learning and living this work our whole lives has inspired us, challenged us, and lent imagination and success to our adventures, art, and businesses. The book provides you with a perspective that's simultaneously wise and enthusiastic, a guidebook by an experienced entrepreneur who values big ideas and the power of storytelling. Krista Anne Nordgren, designer, technologist; Brita Nordgren Wolf, artist, mama, maker; Sarah Rose Nordgren, writer, professor.

All my work is dedicated to my wife Marie, one of the most creative entrepreneurs I know.

My dad had a very creative business career, forging big changes in major business categories three or four times. I watched and learned without realizing how much. Thanks Dad, for show and tell. And especially for the show.

Thanks Kevin, time and again, thanks.

And to JP, a wonderfully creative young man, forever more.

THE GOOD NEWS

I've got good news that I can help you turn into great news.

The good news is that there is a 98 out of a 100 chance that you were born a creative genius.

That's what the research shows.

98% of you born creative genius!

Pretty good odds in your favor, eh?

And the great news is that even if your creatively entrepreneurial qualities have been stunted from lack of use—that same research discovered that by the time we're in our early 30's, only 2% of us are still performing at a creative genius level—well, I'm telling you that they haven't gone away.

With your intentional practice and this book's support and guidance your creatively entrepreneurial talents and abilities will begin to grow today and they will improve steadily as you use them, to serve you in many ways.

So, if your goal is to become the most creatively entrepreneurial version of yourself you can be—and what the heck, why not go bold and fully reclaim your creative genius, it is your natural birthright—then this book is for you.

A Bias for Action is one of the core creative principles informing this book; we'll talk about its importance throughout and you'll be urged to apply your bias for action regularly and immediately, so go ahead and demonstrate it now...

By putting the book down.

And as you think about the idea that being creative and entrepreneurial is core to the human condition, go find evidence in support of it.

And as you do, know you are beginning to work for your creatively entrepreneurial growth.

BORN GENIUSES

Our natural creative genius looks something like this:

When we were young we taught ourselves through the application of tireless curiosity and vigorous and vivid imaginations.

We taught ourselves as we associated ideas or objects we already knew about to create new insights or things we didn't know about.

We didn't just pay attention; we *invested* our attention in the world's offerings and challenges.

When we were very young we exhausted our parents by being creatively entrepreneurial in nearly each inch and just about every minute of our daily lives; we actively created.

Know this: You were a creative genius then, and you delighted in exploring the world through that genius.

Remember?

THE QUANTITATIVE RESEARCH

In the 1960's, back in our wonderfully heroic days of space exploration, NASA knew they would be more successful if they hired more creatively entrepreneurial scientists and engineers. They hired George Land to develop an assessment tool that would measure creative and innovative thinking, and planned to use it during their recruitment processes to identify the best divergent thinkers—divergent thinking is the ability to generate a larger number and a greater variety of options when solving creative problems; divergent thinking is widely appreciated as a core creative cognitive process.

And there's a bunch of ways to measure divergent thinking accurately enough for researchers to be confident in their researched conclusions about it.

When NASA first used the tool to assess those currently working there they were delighted with the results: those known to be most creatively entrepreneurial did the best, and the rest of the results nicely validated what was known about the creative qualities of others. Land was intrigued, and curious, and he decided to use the same tool to assess a representative sample of 1,600 children. They used NASA's grading scale and found that 98% of these kids scored at a genius level. The researchers measured the participants at regular intervals and the test scores rapid retreat as the children grew led the researchers to conclude that non-creative behavior is learned, first and foremost in school.

They concluded being a creative genius defines the human condition.

MY OWN QUALITATIVE RESEARCH

After decades of working as an entrepreneur and creative professional I began teaching courses in creativity and entrepreneurship at Duke University; between 2002 and 2016 I taught over 3,500 students. While Duke Undergrads are in fact extraordinarily successful at accomplishing the challenges school has traditionally, conventionally, been offering, like the rest of us most of them have lost creative genius.

Using the ideas and exercises organized by The Generative Way matrix, nearly 100% of these students were making valuable progress in the growth of their creatively entrepreneurial qualities and abilities in just one semester.

Many experienced immediate and steady growth that was significant.

Since the research shows that the more confident you become the faster your core creative qualities and entrepreneurial instincts will grow, let's consider one more compelling bit of evidence that being creatively entrepreneurial is core to human nature.

Outside of the Western Developed Nations, roughly 70% of all employment is self-generated. Someone finds a problem in the village or neighborhood that can be solved and discovers a way to earn a living—and to feed a family—by solving it.

Without an undergraduate course in Entrepreneurship.

Without any financial capital.

They invest the most generative capital; their inherent creatively entrepreneurial abilities and experiences.

Do you think that makes the case that being creatively entrepreneurial is a truly universal human quality?

If not, why not?

Defining 'Being Creatively Entrepreneurial'

If I ever offer a definition it will be suggestive, and purposefully loose. I've learned while teaching that definitions can result in students believing they've been told what they need to know, so then they stop thinking for themselves, and that's not good.

I hope you agree that it is much better that you have been thinking for yourself about what it is I mean by being creatively entrepreneurial than for me to define it for you the first time I used it?

I'll bet by now you have a very useful understanding that you constructed from what you already know.

So to the understanding of being creatively entrepreneurial that you've been working on, I offer...

It's being generative - producing, building, making, improving, causing.

It's seeing problems as opportunities to make things better and then working at making better things. Or developing better services. Or building better organizations and institutions.

It's looking at what others have looked at and seeing what others missed and understanding how to create advantage from that fresh perspective.

It's adding something extra to the ordinary inches and minutes of daily life.

That's what I mean by being creatively entrepreneurial.

Does that work for you?

What more have you added?

THE GENERATIVE WAY MATRIX

The Generative Way is a matrix designed to help you be and become the most creatively entrepreneurial person you can be.

The Generative Way matrix helps you bring useful organization and efficiency to highly dynamic creatively entrepreneurial concepts and strategies.

The Generative Way matrix is proven successful at helping you think, see, and act like an experienced entrepreneur or creative professional today, and it helps you grow your creatively entrepreneurial qualities and skills steadily.

It is flexible and it is easily applied, regardless of your creatively entrepreneurial development.

I find that folks who are just starting a new commitment to being and becoming the most creatively entrepreneurial person they can be appreciate how immediately useful The Generative Way matrix (TGWay) is.

And that folks who are successful creative professionals appreciate the new insights offered.

After all, Samuel Johnson nailed in way back in the 1700's when he said we don't need to be *informed* as much as we need to be *reminded*.

Creative exercise:

Did you note that I consider TGWay a matrix?

What did that mean to you?

Matrix is a word used precisely by biologists, geologists, chemists, and mathematicians to signify very different things.

Finding all of the advantages of matrix management in business is a creatively entrepreneurial challenge many businesses are taking on.

I am using the meaning the word first had when English speakers adopted and adapted it from the Latin vocabulary—it meant a *fertile womb* in Latin, and its first use in Old English was *any productive place*.

If that's the original meaning of the word matrix, how could that influence how you have been using the word?

WHAT ARE THE SOURCES
OF THE GENERATIVE WAY?

It comes from the best ideas and practices I have learned from…

…25 years of experiences as an entrepreneur and intrapreneur, where I helped start and grow a number of companies across a great range of business categories, including two pioneering cellular telephone companies, two innovative marketing services agencies, a semiconductor business, and a new business incubator that launched another half dozen companies.

…15 years of experiences in four of the creative industries—advertising, book publishing, magazine publishing, and software development.

…for a good portion of what are a combined 35 years it was my job to recruit the most creatively entrepreneurial folks I could find and then help them do their best work—their most generative, most valuable, most profitable work.

…14 years of experiences teaching at Duke University where I've tried out all the best ideas I could find from creatively entrepreneurial leaders and from cutting edge research by neuroscientists and social scientists—and where I learned through playful practice the effective ways to design content offerings that help students grow their generative qualities.

…And it comes from my five years' of experiences as a fishing guide, my first job, when I was still in high school and college and guided for four summers on the English River in Northwestern Ontario and for a winter and summer on the White River in the Arkansas Ozarks.

Being a fishing guide has informed my view of creatively entrepreneurial work always.

Make it your own.

It will serve you best when you turn these concepts into your own.

Pablo Picasso has a great quote on point.

Bad artists borrow, great artists steal.

It took me a while to understand the creatively entrepreneurial wisdom there:

If you are borrowing something you don't own it so you are careful how you use it, constrained and cautious.

But if you *steal* something you've made it your own, and you can use it any way you like.

So steal this content and make it your own. As you read this book, mark it up. Annotate the pages with your own ideas. Play with the exercises. Get physical with it.

And please stop often, get away from the text, and apply one of the concepts you've just read in the work you are doing, or ruminate on another (you could ruminate on what it means to ruminate), or explain one of the ideas you are eager to understand better to someone else, and then apply another.

Whenever you can you want to tap into the wisdom of this proverb.

IF YOU WANT
TO MASTER
SOMETHING
NEW, DON'T
STUDY IT, GET
USED TO IT.

So why not make this guide book your own by filling the blank spaces with your creatively entrepreneurial ideas and expressions.

A prompt: Movement stokes creativity. What does that mean to you?

THE RESEARCH ON WALKING

In a recent study out of Stanford, researchers Oppezzo and Schwartz conducted a series of experiments that demonstrated that walking boosts creativity, in real time and for a short time thereafter. Walking increased 81% of the participants' scores in a divergent thinking creativity test, and 23% of the participants' scores in a convergent thinking creativity test improved.

An easy to benefit from practice: I've long had the discipline of scheduling at least a ten minute walk just before I am going to be engaged in a concerted creative effort, whether delivering a talk, leading a workshop, sitting down to write or working on a project. I appreciate the quality of thinking I do during the walk and feel primed and ready to go when the creative effort begins.

THE GENERATIVE WAY MATRIX

It has a simple organization to it.

The Generative Mindset

- Intentionally Being and Becoming Creatively Entrepreneurial
- Developing and Applying Creative Perspectives
- A Bias for Action

The Generative Toolbox

- Ready-Fire-Aim action strategies
- 4 Generative Behaviors
- Story as a Technology
- Divergent Discovery/Convergent Creation
- The Power of Both
- Servant Leadership

THE GENERATIVE MINDSET

The Generative Mindset is designed to help you develop your own creatively entrepreneurial mindset.

It is built upon three basic principles.

Since each principle is selected and designed to leverage the other two as well as the creatively entrepreneurial strategies in TGWay Toolbox, I plan on introducing each of them to you from multiple angles so you can build the understanding of the principles that is most useful to you.

Intentionally Being And Becoming Creatively Entrepreneurial is the best first principle I have found in my years of searching.

Being intentional is a simple step, one you've taken many times before, every time you determined that there was something worth accomplishing, big or small, every day.

In this case, it begins with your determination, your intention, to be the most creatively entrepreneurial version of yourself you can be—and since you were born a creative genius, your true intention is all it takes for you to begin to grow your creative capacity and develop your entrepreneurial instincts.

A place to be intentional:

I urge my students to start working on this first principle by declaring their intention to themselves.

And an effective place to make that declaration is in the stories we all tell ourselves about ourselves; those stories that capture and frame our expectations for ourselves.

I have found over the years that many and maybe even most folks tell themselves stories about how they really aren't very creative, because they aren't artistic, and that they aren't entrepreneurial, because they haven't started a company.

If that's been your story, change it. And a great way to change it is by immediately acting on your intention and taking on a new creatively entrepreneurial practice, even a modest one.

On the next pages are two that will work hard for you.

Creative Practice 1:

The *30 Day Creative Action Program* (CAP). This exercise will not only demonstrate your intent but is proven to help you grow your creatively entrepreneurial mindset.

The 30 Day CAP is simple and easy to begin; you can start it right now.

Once a day do something you have never done before.

Or

Once a day do something you do regularly, habitually, but do it in a very different way.

It's that simple: Do a brand new activity or do a regular activity in a new fashion, once a day, for a month.

I recommend you identify activities from both categories and that you bring a sense of whimsy, of fun, to your 30 days of activities; a creative mindset needs to be playful.

For example, one of my students kept a list of all the animals she saw one day. Or if you love listening to music but never listen to a particular genre, sit down and listen to a selection from that unfamiliar genre, and listen deeply, fully. Many of my students have done variations on doing a favor for a stranger.

Or the next time you brush your teeth do it with the opposite hand. Or if you always park your car nose first, back in next time.

Some students find their groove right away. A few struggle the first two or three days. By the end of the first week just about all students find this quite engaging.

This exercise is based on the work of Dr. James Kaufman when he was at California State University, in San Bernardino; currently he's at the University of Connecticut. His research is clear: a 30 Day CAP will make a measurable improvement to your creative mindset, to your natural abilities for divergent and convergent creative thinking.

Have fun as you are intentionally being creatively entrepreneurial!

You can start today…and you might want to record your thoughts along the way by keeping a journal.

May 25th

~ Cut through the woods on today's bike ride. Saw a fox and a beautiful kind of bird I've never noticed before (remember to look up).

~ Took my laptop out of the office and worked outside for the day. Idea: sun shades for laptop screens.

May 26th

~ Tried Lebanese food for the first time! Must try a second time and a third...

May 27th

~ Saw a train parked by the road on the way home, stopped to look at all the graffiti. How do they get their colors and lines so sharp??

Creative Practice 2:

Your *Generative Journal.* Here's another exercise that is easy to do. And it's a favorite with my students.

Keeping a journal is a simple discipline to commit to regular use, and because your natural creatively entrepreneurial qualities are ready to be rekindled, you get great results quickly when you develop your creatively entrepreneurial ideas and questions in a journal.

My students find their journals to be a valuable early opportunity to 'let your freak flag fly' and really let loose with creative riffs and entrepreneurial rambles, learning important lessons: to stop editing themselves and that developing creative ideas is most effective when it is fun.

Here's just one way your journal entries payoff: It takes a certain understanding of a creative idea or entrepreneurial thought to hold it in your head. It takes a different sort of understanding of an idea to write it down. And it takes another type of understanding of an idea to visually represent it.

This is a very important early lesson, to surround an idea, and to get used to it, to explore its full complex pattern.

So instead of just thinking your creative thoughts and wondering about your entrepreneurial ideas in your head, write them down.

Then I urge you to work on visual representations of them.

Graphs, doodles, maps, drawings, they are all useful when considering your ideas.

Think about it. Write about it. Visualize it. Each step reveals something new.

Begin to play with visuals right away—I require my students make the second week of the semester 'visual entry week' with all entries visual—and my website has a list of resources for quick tutorials and tips on the basics of visual thinking.

And if you hesitate at being visual in your journal because that story you tell yourself about not being creative has a chapter titled "I can't draw", Bill Fick, a part time Duke prof and full-time graphic artist, illustrator, and cartoonist says "Trust the intelligence in your hand. Bring the pencil to the paper and set aside your judgment and just see what happens."

And make that a colored pencil and see how that influences your expressions.

As you practice doing this in your journal, as you play with your ideas from all their angles, soon you are doing it naturally, as part of your intentionally creatively entrepreneurial mindset.

Especially if you are having fun trying.

Do you want a journal that's compact and easy to carry, that's always with you? Do you want a large format journal so you can mark boldly at your desk at the end of the day?

Don't keep this journal digitally. There are a bunch of research findings about how important it is to be holding something in your hand to fully engage your creative capacity.

I believe that just as a pen or pencil lead makes an imprint on the page when you make a mark, writing with a pen or a pencil makes an imprint on your mind.

And you are keyboarding your thoughts and ideas all the time. Do something different with your journal, and you are on your way to thinking differently.

I offer my students some prompts for journal entries that will accelerate your creatively entrepreneurial development.

- Keep a look out for expressions and examples of creatively entrepreneurial behavior that seem to be in any way generative. What happens in the moment when folks are, for instance, generous in their response to a situation? When you see it, think about it, then write a quick riff about it.

- Be mindful of good and bad design. When a product feels just right, or clunky wrong, think about why that is, then write it down, or visually represent your experience with it. And services are designed too, so when a store is not handling customers well, think about the improvement that could be made and make it an entry in your journal.

- When you learn of a great business strategy or story line or generative idea, don't just admire it, learn from it. Write down or map why it's a great idea.

- And listen for interesting language, and wonder what it was that caught your attention when it does. Similes and metaphors are fun to listen for—they each help us understand A by declaring its relationship to B, a useful creatively entrepreneurial talent.

I require my students make a minimum of three entries a week.

Part of my evaluation of my students' journals is the answer to the question "does it look like a creative mind was hanging out there and having fun?" Seems like that's a good self-evaluation.

If you are determined to not just grow your creatively entrepreneurial qualities but reclaim you creative genius, do both of these creative exercises together. Start journaling as you begin your 30 Day CAP.

They will reinforce each other, accelerating and strengthening your growth.

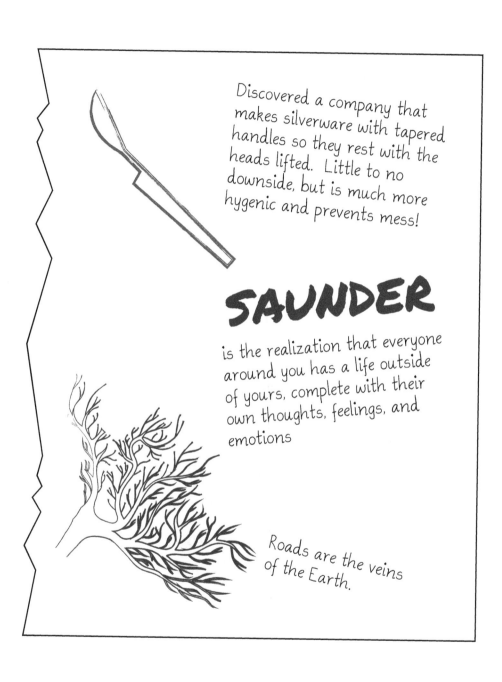

Discovered a company that makes silverware with tapered handles so they rest with the heads lifted. Little to no downside, but is much more hygenic and prevents mess!

SAUNDER

is the realization that everyone around you has a life outside of yours, complete with their own thoughts, feelings, and emotions

Roads are the veins of the Earth.

So first you declared your creatively entrepreneurial intentions to yourself.

Then you took action in support of your declaration.

And once you believe your commitment is true and your intention is real—then you *should* declare your intention to others.

Yes, you *should* declare to others that you are a creatively entrepreneurial person.

The change in your creatively entrepreneurial mindset that occurs when a true declaration is made, and the change in how the world considers you, taps into ancient wisdoms.

The Scottish mountaineer, H.W. Murray, wrote:

"Concerning all acts of initiative and creation there is one elementary truth, the ignorance of which kills countless ideas and splendid plans: that the moment one definitely commits oneself, then Providence moves too. All sorts of things occur to help one that would never otherwise have occurred. A whole stream of events issues from the decision, raising in one's favor all manner of unforeseen incidents and meetings and material assistance, which no

*man could have dreamed would
have come his way. Whatever you
can do, or dream you can do, begin
it. Boldness has genius, power, and
magic in it. Begin it now."*

I have found time and again that my intentionally bold creatively entrepreneurial action generates a productive reaction; the networks that I am just starting to build when I act on my interest in exploring something new will begin to serve my discovery sooner than later— folks begin to reach out to me through these new networks, for instance.

So when you tell the world that from now on you are going to be the most creatively entrepreneurial person you can be, the world begins to treat you that way, reinforcing your efforts and bringing new opportunity to grow.

"What you think, you become."
-BUDDHA

There's even more generative benefit coming from declaring your intention to be and become creatively entrepreneurial, and it's an immediate benefit.

For centuries the great religions have known of the importance of requiring their novitiates to declare their intentions to believe in the teachings and sacred truths of their religion; they know that in that moment of intentional declaration of faith that those novices begin to see the world differently, in a fashion shaped by and consistent with their faith narrative.

It's an insight captured by the author, Anais Nin.

"WE DON'T SEE
THINGS AS
THEY ARE; WE
SEE THEM AS
WE ARE."

- ANAIS NIN, AUTHOR

So when you leverage your new creatively entrepreneurial practices with a public declaration of your intention, you immediately begin to see the world as a creatively entrepreneurial person sees the world, *and* increasingly you are treated that way by the world.

Of course the difference in your view of the world initially is likely incremental, but notice I didn't write *only* incremental, for that increment is very important.

You can't overestimate the importance of the *increment* in your creatively entrepreneurial development and in your work.

In praise of the increment:

As you grow your creatively entrepreneurial qualities you anticipate that you are more likely to discover the big bold transformative idea that changes the game, and yes, that's so.

However, the generation of a transformative idea is rare in even the most creative folks' lives—you influence it but have no control over it.

But what you can control as an intentionally creatively entrepreneurial person is the increment: how you inform the inches and the minutes of daily life with your generative thoughts and actions.

Imagine how you would do that, and what it would mean, if you were determined to offer just a little bit more creative expression as you attend to the details.

That can be as transformative as any game changing idea, and *you can intentionally control that.*

Now imagine a company filled with creatively entrepreneurial folks intentionally informing the inches and minutes of daily organizational life with generative thoughts and actions.

What would that look like in your organization?

What can you do to inform the next increment with a creatively entrepreneurial energy or a generative performance?

How will you next be intentionally creatively entrepreneurial?

The second principle of The Generative Mindset is *Developing your Creative Perspectives.*

Notice it's Perspectives: It's important to accentuate the plural *s* so that immediately we see we must always strive for multiple points of view for every creative problem or entrepreneurial opportunity.

You want to be able to look at what you have been looking at and see it in a totally new way. You are most likely to accomplish that if you try on many vantage points.

The TGWay Toolbox has a number of strategies and concepts to help you develop and apply a range of creative perspectives; here we attend to the underlying principle to help you create your creatively entrepreneurial mindset, one that invites your most useful creative perspectives.

Creativity is a numbers game so you want as many perspectives on a problem or opportunity as you can get.

That's so important—intentionally applying *many* creative perspectives—that it will be reinforced again and again.

The same path looks quite different depending on which way you are walking it, and where you started it, and who your companions are, and where you think it's taking you.

Just an incremental change in your creative perspectives may lead to the insight that makes a world of difference in your understanding of the opportunity.
When developing and applying your creative perspectives, be aware of the *primacy effect's* influence. The first thought you have about a new

object or idea, or what you experience in the first moments visiting a new place, will impact and sometimes even define how you see it or think about it thereafter.

Whether that first impression from one perspective is useful or not, you don't want it to be the only impression.

The first new idea you come up with when you are trying to solve a creative problem or develop an entrepreneurial opportunity will have a primacy effect influence and maybe even direct your subsequent thinking unless you intentionally set that first new idea aside—for now—and intentionally start again with new creative perspectives.

The first idea will be there if you can't come up with an improvement, and the new perspectives you tried on to generate more options are very likely to give you fresh insights into your first idea.

So be mindful of the primacy effect, and look out for a member of its extended family, *functional fixedness* —when we use an object over and over for a specific purpose we lose our capacity to see that object in any other context—as you intentionally take on a variety of creatively entrepreneurial perspectives.

If I am in a playful mood when someone asks me what I do for a living I tell folks my job is I help everyone become deviants.

After a pause I modify it.

My job is to help people become *creative deviants*.

Think of being a creative deviant as intentionally viewing the opportunity or the challenge or the product or the company from every angle—as an advocate and as a contrarian, up and down, inside and out, today and tomorrow, coming and going, in red and in black, alert and tired, taking it seriously and laughing at it, in the office and in the woods—trying out the perspectives others don't try so you can see what no one else, including you, has previously seen.

Laughing at least some of the time, and intentionally having fun most of the time, will help.

QUALITATIVE RESEARCH

That we are born creatively entrepreneurial and that we are naturally inclined to appreciate the value of many perspectives when figuring out a challenge was demonstrated by my then two-year-old granddaughter as I watched her first experience using a traditional hand-cranked apple peeler. A woman brought my granddaughter to it, with an apple already on the spindle, and my granddaughter was fascinated to watch the real time results as the woman guided her turning the handle to make the apple rotate against the blade, creating a ribbon of peel.

Then the woman removed the peeled apple and my granddaughter leaned in even closer and carefully and deliberately touched each and every part of the peeler, from the base to the blade, the threaded pin and the cam; she seemed compelled to. Then as a second little girl set up and peeled her apple my granddaughter slowly walked all around the scene, investing her attention in what was happening from every angle.

That's a nice picture of developing creative perspectives. Get so close you can touch it, smell it, taste it, then step back, then walk all around it.

And don't pay attention; *invest* your attention.

It's also a picture of our natural creative genius—no one taught my granddaughter to behave that way.

The second second principle—please take a moment to appreciate that this is the *second* second principle of The Generative Mindset—is a *Bias For Action*.

Being Intentionally Creatively Entrepreneurial is the first of the principles, for intention is needed from the start. *Developing your Creative Perspectives* and a *Bias for Action* dance together, (being intentional plays the tune) one leading the other and then changing places.

I hope you have been following the book's lead from the beginning and are already applying your own bias for action, which is what a successful creatively entrepreneurial person knows to do, to take action, to make something happen, as soon as you can.

To help your bias for action be most effective at the start of a creative project or entrepreneurial initiative, TGWay Toolbox offers Ready Fire Aim action strategies to guide your first steps.

In this section I'll help you develop your own thoughts about how a bias for action serves your creatively entrepreneurial mindset.

DISCOVERING
WHAT YOU
SHOULD   >   PREDICTING
CREATE   WHAT YOU
                       WILL CREATE

And you are doing yourself a big big favor if
you put the book aside and think about why
that might be and find examples of the truth
of it in your work and your life before you read
on.

THE CORPORATE WAY

Many of us are convinced that when we are starting a creative or entrepreneurial project that will bring something new into existence that we must begin by producing The Plan of what we are going to do and how we will do it.

Producing The Plan is the first step corporations take and it's been their model for a long, long time; it is a practice most other institutions—schools, non-profits, governments—and many individuals have taken up.

It seems a necessary practice in corporations, this immediate production of The Plan. Because a corporation of any size has many creative initiatives and projects underway all the time, each one needs a budget; fiscal responsibility demands it.

Well, to establish an accurate budget, each project needs to develop The Plan of what is to be built or developed and the resources needed to create it.

That means that when the team is most ignorant about what they could be doing—an ignorance that always exists at the start of a project—they have to *predict* what they are going to build or develop so they can produce The Plan to arrive at the budget, so they can get started.

But all of the environments and communities and markets where opportunities are found and things are built are *highly complex*; that means the dynamics of every opportunity are constantly changing, always becoming something else, while the prediction and The Plan provides us with a static view that was ill-formed in the first place.

The Plan is a road map based on a prediction of the terrain we've never visited, at best only read about, and it plots a road we must follow even though the terrain is constantly shifting, always changing.

On complexity: Systems and networks and organizations are considered to be complex when they are made up of independent entities that are continually adapting to each other; each adaptation adds to the unpredictable nature of complex systems; as the relationships between these entities change, so does the whole.

Show your bias for action by again putting down the book and going for a walk to gain new perspective on the creative problem or new opportunity you are working on right now.

To get your thoughts going you might want to look for examples of complexity.

Nature, everywhere you see it, is the result of local relationships between a great array of entities—seen and unseen—that adapt to each other and become larger systems.

Watch for that.

Cities are made up of many bottoms-up self-generated communities, defined by geography or by interests. What does that look like? How does that work?

What bottoms up self-organization occurs in your company or school or institution?

It's true that more and more innovative corporations are challenging the tightest strictures of the predictive model, and so this riff on the role of The Plan as de facto standard in corporate innovation is a bit overstated. But seeing this fundamental disadvantage created by The Plan serves as a useful contrast to how experienced and successful entrepreneurs and creative professionals set out *discovering* what they will create, rather than making a prediction they are then stuck with.

When skilled creatively entrepreneurial professionals want to develop the most useful understanding of a new opportunity, they don't study it, *they get used to it.* And you get used to it through action, with it, amongst it, as part of it, touching and feeling and smelling it.

So a Bias for Action energy runs through all the elements of The Generative Mindset to help you make your way from effective discovery through to value-added execution.

A conventional "Ready, Aim, Fire" attitude makes The Plan the priority.

But TGWay flips the last two steps to make it *Ready, Fire, Aim* because that's the most useful approach to quickly getting started at discovering what it is you want to accomplish, so you get to invest attention to what is happening as you act, and then you get to take next steps informed by the new insights you've just gained.

That quick and early calibration is progress.

And it generates the most useful intelligence.

Ready Fire Aim appreciates that a body at rest tends to stay at rest but a body in motion tends to stay in motion and that building something of value is a momentum play.

Sure you need to analyze. But the most useful analysis comes as or after you have taken action.

Fire, *then* you get a smarter Aim for your next step.

In fact analysis is so important to your creatively entrepreneurial work that you need to continually analyze all along the way.

So when you have an interest, or an inclination, or a gut feeling about an opportunity, Ready Fire Aim says act on it.

So you can learn something about it. And think about what you are learning as you keep it up.

President Theodore Roosevelt understood action as well anyone.

"DO WHAT YOU CAN, WITH WHAT YOU HAVE, WHERE YOU ARE."

- THEODORE ROOSEVELT, AMERICAN PRESIDENT

More on Complexity

A few more thoughts about Complexity and
your creatively entrepreneurial mindset's
bias for action:

Complicated isn't the same as complex.

A clockworks is complicated - it is made up
of many pieces, but none of them can adapt,
they are what they are, so when you remove
one piece the clock is broken and it no longer
works.

New Orleans is complex, made up of many
entities that are continually adapting to each
other and to outside stimuli, so when the
city is smacked down so hard by Hurricane
Katrina it is nearly destroyed the pieces
that survived adapted and a new whole re-
emerges.

The opposite of complicated is simple.

The opposite of complex is singular.

Your creative and entrepreneurial actions
will be taking place in markets and

organizations and environments that are all complex, every one of them.

There are some powerfully generative concepts you want simmering in your creative mindset that complexity scientists are helping us understand.

These concepts help us see some of the compounding energies and high leverage growth strategies often available in complex environments.

Like Bottoms-Up Self-Organization, the healthiest growth, because the intelligence guiding the growth is distributed throughout the system, because the growth is rooted in the self-interests of the participants, and because the whole is always becoming what it needs to be next.

And Phase Changes, where a complex system absorbs outside inputs with little or no effect until the next increment added is the one that transforms the system into something else. This was popularized by Malcolm Gladwell as tipping points.

And Networked Positive Feedback Loops - the most common is what we call "going viral" - that can propel an idea or a behavior or a unit across a system.

As you grow your creatively entrepreneurial genius back again, spending some time intentionally reading about, and looking for, and playing with complexity concepts will tune up your mindset nicely to begin to plug into those energies naturally.

I am always in pursuit of sustainable abundance in my creatively entrepreneurial efforts and the forces of complexity, relying heavily on the strategy of bottoms up self-organization, have created sustainable abundance in nature time and again.

I invite you to think about what sustainable abundance means before I share some of my thoughts.

For now be clear that TGWay matrix presumes a complex world of constant and often unpredictable change.

THE GENERATIVE TOOLBOX

The Generative Toolbox is a set of strategically generative concepts and strategies that will have a fundamental impact on you being and becoming the most creatively entrepreneurial person you can be.

Playing with them, getting used to them, and applying them will help restore your birthright creative genius.

When I first labeled this section of the matrix I called it the The Generative Toolkit. I soon realized that not only is tool box a much better analogy, tool kit is actually wrong.

Wonder for a moment why tool kit is wrong.

It's wrong because you are making this content your own, you are creating your own matrix of creatively entrepreneurial concepts that work for you, and a toolkit is a defined set of tools, so specific and so limited that the case a toolkit comes in is often molded or die cut to offer a particular place for a specific tool.

A toolbox is open and easily adapted to your needs; you make it your own by adding to it as you choose.

No two carpenters' toolboxes are alike, but most of them have a hammer and a saw, screw drivers and a wrench, a level and a tape measure.

And while no two creative genius' toolboxes are the same, The Generative Toolbox starts you off with the basic tools most useful for most of us most of the time—useful as you grow your creatively entrepreneurial talents and abilities, and useful as you get creative and entrepreneurial work done.

Use them as you please.

READY FIRE AIM

Is ready fire aim part of your creative mindset yet?

Have you embraced the idea, in a form that is working for you, that regardless of whether the new project was assigned, or you chose it, or it chose you, you should get started just as soon as you can?

That you should get started discovering what you should build, and then you are *continually planning* as you are building it.

Has anyone ever faced a more complex operational challenge than Winston Churchill did during World War II? What incredible logistics.

Well, he was clear about the value of The Plan when he said:

"Plans are of little importance, but planning is essential."

You will improve your chances of success in all your creative and entrepreneurial work when you get your subconscious mind working for you. So an additional and very important reason to get started right away on your creatively entrepreneurial work is that when you start it you are in effect making another declaration— that this project is now important to you—and making that declaration so impresses this project into your conscious mind that it also impresses the project into your subconscious mind.

Since your subconscious mind can process over 20 million bits of information in the same brief moment of time your conscious mind processes 40, and since your subconscious mind is always alert, constantly and continuously engaged in pattern recognition and trying new mash-ups and exploring fresh associations, then getting your subconscious mind working on your project for you is an important early accomplishment.

By starting a project with enough committed boldness, your subconscious goes to work, checking each and every new input against your experiences and knowledge bases and interests, until something interesting is found.

If I start a new project with sufficient vigor and then leave it for a couple of weeks to attend to more immediate matters, it's not unusual to find a useful new idea waiting for me when I return.

And your subconscious is all the more effectively at work for you when you don't just study a new opportunity, but rather when you get used to it.

Ready Fire Aim helps you to get used to the new opportunity or challenge that faces you as you discover what you should be creating. It directs your energy towards productive behavior.

These RFA action strategies will guide you as part of your personal development efforts—developing your creatively entrepreneurial qualities on your way to regaining your creative genius—and they can guide you when you are working on a new project or facing a new challenge.

Wondering While Wandering comes first—it's a good way to start.

What first thoughts come to mind when you read Wondering While Wandering?

What's the first creative or entrepreneurial or generative benefit that you can imagine coming from wondering while wandering?

"THE
BEGINNING
OF WISDOM IS
WONDER, AND
THE BEGINNING
OF WONDER IS
AWE."

- ABRAHAM HESCHEL, A LEADING JEWISH
THEOLOGIAN, 1907 TO 1972

Experienced entrepreneurs and creative professionals spend a lot of time wondering while wandering because it is their nature, their predisposition; they are regularly exploring interesting places and constantly searching for better questions to ask.

And since the goal is to get started right away and get started right, then wondering while wandering midst the issues and the elements, the places and the people, the questions and the changes that make up your new opportunity or big challenge, is the easiest and most effective way to start.

After all, there's not much that's easier than wandering.

And wondering while wandering is effective, right off; it sets you up to look at what you have been looking at and now see what you haven't seen before.

The open-ended and circuitous searching that comes of wandering, while continually wondering about the new questions to ask of what you are seeing and experiencing, this increases the chances you will come upon the right opportunity from a new angle with a creatively smart question.

Another useful aspect of seeing your first Ready Fire Aim steps as wondering while wandering is that the language of it invites some playfulness. Playful perspectives can be very creative ones, often leading to the most useful insights.

And wandering sounds like you're moving on, which is good, but wandering can also result in you doubling back which is often very good, as you then have new perspectives on what you've already seen, and more experiences to reflect on.

Wondering while wandering is playful, but it's not aimless. You are purposeful, in that you are always alert.

Alert to where your interests are challenged.

Alert to where your needs are met.

Alert to new questions that you don't have answers for.

Alert to where your talents or your experiences are useful.

And always alert for the evidence of a *sustainable abundance*. I didn't call it that back when I was most actively an entrepreneur, but I was looking for an indication of it.

I know I still haven't explained what I think sustainable abundance means. I think there is such an important idea there that I want all of us to be thinking about what it could mean in our generative work before I share my sense of it.

Wondering while wandering is a state of mind, but it is also a course of action. Please embrace the research out of Stanford that I introduced on page 16 that showed how much more creative we are when we walk.

And when you are walking, hold something in your hand. Like an early prototype you are playing with or some representative icon of the issue at hand. Research shows that when you have something in your hand, when you engage your sense of touch, your creative mind is more active.

RFA STRATEGY 2:
FIND FRIENDS FAST

Be alert for new friends while wandering.

Who is asking the most interesting questions about your new interest or opportunity?

Have you introduced yourself?

Creatively entrepreneurial work is collaborative work so be on the lookout for others with similar or complimentary interests, or with interesting vantage points, or with influence.

And when you find friends who are living creatively entrepreneurial lives, spending time with them will help you grow your creatively entrepreneurial abilities. Some call it a virtuous circle, and all within it are served by it.

Look for friends you can leverage and look for those who can leverage you.

Look for new friends among your old friends, by discovering a new relationship.

Announcing to the world that you've begun your discovery efforts for a new creative or entrepreneurial project or that you have set out to reclaim your creative genius will often result in new friends finding you.

And when you do for others what you would like them to do for you, when you show these first friends that you are genuinely interested in helping them with their creative discovery, you are growing strong ties that becomes a generative network of strategic allies.

RFA STRATEGY 3:
FAIL FAST, FAIL OFTEN, FAIL CHEAP

It's been the hot entrepreneurial mantra for a few years now, and it won't ever go away, there is so much wisdom to it.

It means different things according to your circumstance—hardware development is vastly different than software development, for instance—but it always means that you should get started, because first among your early objectives when you set out to create something new is your need to become very knowledgeable about your new opportunity or challenge very fast.

So you make a first quick move based on what you know now, or based on an opportunity or a hunch, don't worry which, because there are no missteps, you learn as much in these earliest days when things go wrong as when they go right, so you want lots and lots of these little forays, or experiments, or both, where you are only making a misstep if you fail to learn something from them.

Fail fast doesn't just mean get started fast. It also means look for trials or projects you can conclude quickly, so you can analyze the information and consider its importance sooner than later, and determine there is more here to develop or you should move on.

FF/FO/FC respects the idea that creativity is a numbers game—a great idea most likely is found when you have explored many, the best solution will be revealed when you have considered a range of options—and so you need to respect the important or scarce resources you have under your control at the start because you are going to invest them energetically.

Don't spend your resources, invest them.

And how can you leverage them?

Is there a friend who can do complimentary projects or experiments?

As an investment, you look for a return.

One important return on your investment is all this great proprietary knowledge you are creating. Quickly, you know something that others don't, because you were there and they weren't.

It's your creative capital, and you want to grow it fast.

And you're getting used to your opportunity when you are applying FF/FO/FC.

As you keep trying new ideas or strategies and analyzing your results, you'll be looking for patterns in the challenges.

Or anomalies in the opportunity.

Or confluences between those patterns and those anomalies.

Or need for your skills and interests.

Or other dynamics that begin to frame your opportunity, that find an early focus or early handle.

Don't ever look at these early efforts as failing; at the least it's research, but it's also important progress.

Thomas J. Watson, the Chairman and CEO of IBM through most of the first half of the 20th century as it grew into an international giant, said:

"THE WAY TO SUCCEED IS TO DOUBLE YOUR ERROR RATE."

- THOMAS J. WATSON, CHAIRMAN AND CEO OF IBM

RFA STRATEGY 4:
CROSS THE BOUNDARIES, FISH THE CONFLUENCES

As you are looking for new creative perspectives on the opportunity or problem that faces you, a good direction for your wandering is over there, in unfamiliar places, in the parts of your company, or town, or marketplace, or technology, or school, that are other than where you are at or what you know today or what you are doing now.

This provides you with another of the many creative perspectives you need and maybe one of the most important.

The others' perspectives.

This also serves you as you work at reclaiming your creative genius. The wider your interests and the more diverse your experiences, the more creative your thinking will be when approaching a challenge.

Think of the benefits that come from considering your problem from unfamiliar ground.

Please, take a few minutes to think about all the benefits.

So what are you going to do about it?

And it's important to have strategic allies and friends in places you're not.

Another good place to look for opportunity or insight into an issue or problem is where communities and systems and standards and markets and habits and habitats meet, overlap, intersect, or collide.

Wander and wonder where things are handed off, from one to another.

Where in your organization does that happen?

Wonder and wander where ideas are bumping into each other.

Where in your network of friends and associates is that occurring?

Wonder and wander where things are transitioning, and becoming something else.

Where is that emergence happening in your life?

Have you noticed how the forest is interesting, the meadow is too, but it's where they meet that the most diverse expressions of life occur?

When Rivers Meet

I guided on the White River in Arkansas, on the stretch of that river below Bull Shoals Dam; the river was fed water from the bottom of Bull Shoals Lake so it was cold enough for hatchery raised rainbow and brown trout, fish that thrive in cooler waters. If we went on a two-day float trip down the river we arrived at the place where the Buffalo River, one of our last wild rivers, flowed into the White. The Buffalo is a natural warm water river, with outstanding smallmouth bass fishing. My guests had great fishing where the two rivers met, catching a rainbow trout on one cast, a bass on the next.

An Other Creative Exercise:

Find reasons to wander on the other side of where you spend most of your time right now. Go wander and wonder in a different department of your organization. Go wander and wonder on the customers' premises, in and around the customers' world.

Or at a key vendor or supplier.

Before you go, think about what you would like to know.

Once you are there, and start wandering, forget the questions you brought with you and look for new ones.

One question that might help you find new ones: What is it that is different in this other place, and why is that?

Why? is quite often the most important question. Why is that?

RFA STRATEGY 5:
LOOK FOR THE BALL ON THE 10 YARD LINE.

Doesn't it make sense that you will find it easier to be opportunistic without the restrictions of The Plan?

The prediction that led to The Plan will shape what you are looking at which can prevent you from even noticing the easy win that could lead you in a generative direction you could and maybe should be developing.

Creating advantage from your early easy victory helps you gain momentum for all of what you want to accomplish.

RFA STRATEGY 6:
CLIMATE CONTROL NOT COMMAND AND CONTROL.

Because complex systems are so adaptive, so dynamic, they are usually unpredictable in their response to changes, whether internal or external, and sometimes wildly so. That means that, over time and in most circumstances, a command and control leadership approach to your discovery efforts won't be as effective as a climate control leadership approach.

That means that you should never assume you can demand the precise thing happen that you are counting on; instead you want to influence all the conditions that you can to work in your favor when you can, so your preferred outcome is most likely to emerge.

This seems particularly effective when leading creatively entrepreneurial organizations.

Rather than demand a particular outcome, I tried to manage the circumstances and influence the environment to make it most likely that what I wanted the organization to accomplish is what the organization wanted to accomplish and was aligned to accomplish effectively.

So, while wondering and wandering, identify those conditions you can influence.

MORE READY FIRE AIM

Some further insights into an effective Ready Fire Aim approach to accomplishing creative and entrepreneurial work include:

Planning > The Plan

The Generative Way Matrix and your bias for action put planning in place of The Plan.

When you discover what should be done, when you discover the most promising development strategy for the opportunity, and it is time to design it and build it, you must be planning in service of the work you are doing.

And as you continue to make your way, you will continue planning in service of the next phase of work you are doing.

Plann*ing* supports the work you discover you should be doing to create the product, develop the service, build the organization.

The risk is that the prediction is from the wrong vantage point and then sticking to The Plan restricts or even prevents the best work.

Trust your gut.

I always thought that was a useful analogy for how I experience the creative intuition of my subconscious, and I was always inclined to trust it even before I learned how much data the subconscious is continually processing for me.

Now we know the same neuropeptides found in our brains that scientists have long associated with thinking are found in our gut as well.

You have creative intelligences all throughout your body and you want to trust them, you want to use them all.

Look for the important questions well before you worry about answers.

Asking the best questions earlier than later drives a project towards success.

You will find a whole section of our website dedicated to helping you find the best questions.

They all point to: Ask lots of Why? questions.

WONDER
& CONSIDER
& ASK
& EXAMINE
& RUMINATE
& WONDER.

4 GENERATIVE BEHAVIORS

The Generative Toolbox offers you four generative behaviors to practice as part of your commitment to recovering your natural born creative genius.

When these behaviors begin to shape your daily approach to life—as you intentionally practice them in the inches and the minutes—your creative capacity grows, your entrepreneurial instincts develop.

And when you are focusing on a project, a creative initiative, a piece of new work, then intentionally applying these behaviors to your ready fire aim actions will support your success.

These 4 generative behaviors were chosen because they are simple, they reward you immediately, and they reward you in many ways.

BEING GENEROUS.

This behavior is seminal to TGWay matrix.

I like pragmatic altruism—when the strategically smart move has an inherent goodness to it—it's creative and it's so often so easy.

Being generous is a core example of pragmatic altruism, since your generosity will bring forth a generous response from others.

Maybe not 100% of the time, but it's another smart bet, a smart generative bet, that it will work in your favor most of the time.

And doesn't that sound like a creative success, to be in a generous relationship with another?

Being generous enriches your creative mindset and it will cause the people around you to become more generative in your favor.

Again, not all the time. But it's the best bet.

What does it look like to be in a generous relationship with the people you work with?

What does it look like to be in a generous relationship with the marketplace?

Isn't there the promise of growing reward when you are in a generous relationship with the marketplace?

Could that lead to something like sustainable abundance?

Being Generous is Being Generative:

It's true. Just look at them, they're basically the same word. They share the same Latin root, genero.

The dictionaries I checked translate genero as the verb to beget, to produce...and to create.

One way to practice being generous I urge my students to take up is to become known for giving what must be the greatest gift of all these days, their undivided attention, and practice being generous listeners.

That means focused listening, blocking out all distractions, and putting your phone away.

And it also means carefully listening, for the best the idea has to offer.

Generous listening is *appreciative*.

It's the attitude of intentionally appreciating what is being said. And it listens for ways to help the idea appreciate in value.

Can we agree that a brand new idea is most often a fragile thing, filled with holes and incapable of standing on its own? It's so easy to deflate it, even dismiss it; simply demanding more of it than it has had time to develop can be fatal to the life of a young idea.

So avoid the temptation of being the smartest person in the room, rushing to tell everything wrong with the idea, for you just might kill it.

Instead, listen carefully for the best the idea has to offer; see it in its most promising form.

When you do the return on your investment is very generous.

Careful listening results in the idea impressing your subconscious, and as your subconscious does its thing, immediately searching for interesting relationships between this new idea and your experiences and your understandings, you are exercising your creative mind, and your care-filled listening means you are absorbing this new idea, its context and content, so it will be there for your future reference.

Steve Jobs said creativity is just connecting the dots so you should make sure you have lots of dots. That's what careful and generous listening does for you right off. It's an easy way to collect more dots.

You become more adept in your creative thinking and you add to the richness of your resources.

The best thinking about your friend's idea now informs your own; some element of your friend's idea may later be an important piece for your own work.

That's an immediate return on your investment of your generous attention.

After you have listened carefully for the best the idea has to offer the first questions you are likely to ask and the first things you're likely to say to your friend are shaped by your generous consideration, making it more likely what you say will enhance the idea, appreciating the best version of it at that stage of its development.

You'll make friends fast if you keep helping them improve their ideas.

Another potential return on the intentional investment of your generous attention is you could become known as the person to go to when someone has a new idea. That's a great place to be in an organization, where the new ideas are being tried out.

And perhaps your generous behavior catches on, and your organization or group of friends gets better, even if only incrementally, at inviting folks to share new ideas for solving problems or making better things.

Finally, after demonstrating to your friends that you see the best in their ideas and even try to help improve them, you are now on the most solid common ground you can stand on to provide the tough critique of the idea your friend needs to hear, when needed, if needed.

If you have useful challenges to offer, they are delivered and received most productively after you've demonstrated your generous approach to their ideas.

BEING HUMBLE.

Please don't confuse being humble with being meek and mild.

You can be proud of your accomplishments and still be humble in your person.

In fact, it's quite attractive, watching a humble person experience the natural pride that comes from solving a problem or learning something new.

But what's the creative benefit, the entrepreneurial benefit, from intentionally practicing humility?

You'll find your answer as you think about these questions.

Can you accept that right now you don't know much of what you will need to know to succeed at your next challenge?

Can you accept that most of your first attempts at accomplishing something new won't turn out as you expected?

Can you accept that you have to ask a lot of questions others will consider foolish on your way to finding the best questions to ask?

Do you understand that the best authority isn't demanded; it's the authority granted?

That's the humility of TGWay matrix, the humility that is so important to growing your creative capacity and discovering the best creative perspectives and entrepreneurial strategies for solving the problem you're currently facing.

It's the humility that allows you to carefully listen to others, and to genuinely serve others.

BEING PLAYFUL.

For years my students were required to identify a piece of research from neuroscientists or behavioral scientists about creativity or entrepreneurship, and then tell the class what the practical benefits of the research are to those of us trying to regain our creative genius.

There is a common conclusion found in the majority of the neuroscience research projects: you become more creative when you can take on a new mindset, other than your status quo operating mode.

And one of the most effective ways to get into a new mindset, in the moment, is to be playful.

That allows you to see the problem as a game and the challenge as a chance to play at working it out.

Child's play—the games children are making up as they are playing them— isn't about winning or losing.

It's about discovering what happens now and might happen next.

When children play the games they create they are rarely keeping score.

So there's little concern about failing.

That's what allows imagination free rein to reign.

Playfulness lets them turn a stumble into a skip until they can run again.

When children play the story keeps emerging and so a cloth is a cape until it needs to be a sail and a stick is a sword until it's broken in half to be a telescope.

Something much like that often happens in the early development of a new project. The piece you build now for one purpose might need to become something else as the project matures.

Children don't have to study complexity to get used to what creative emergence feels like as it is happening; they literally play with it.

Research also shows what we've known for centuries but too often forget: The best way to learn is through play.

You certainly get used to something if you are playing with it.

You develop the aptitude for continuous improvement and the entrepreneurial instinct of rapid prototyping through child's play.

Why is that?

All creators, producers, entrepreneurs, builders, developers, are making it up as they go along.

Which is as it must be.

When I was starting companies my partners and I spoke of the challenge of building something new as learning to fly the airplane as we were figuring out how to build it, and building the airplane we were learning to fly.

That sort of challenge shares important qualities with open-ended child's play.

As already introduced and reinforced here, creativity is a numbers game.

"THE BEST WAY TO HAVE A GOOD IDEA IS TO HAVE LOTS OF IDEAS."

- LINUS PAULING, NOBEL PRIZE CHEMISTRY, 1954, NOBEL PEACE PRIZE, 1962.

When you bring a sense of fun to your creative efforts, you won't be in a hurry to finish up by grabbing hold of the first decent idea that comes along…you're having too much fun, you want to keep playing.

So you try out more ideas, different ideas, making it more likely you discover the best idea.

Being playful often leads to new creative perspectives, both in idea generation and in executional development.

TO THE MILLENNIAL GENERATION

Yours is the first generation that didn't get to fill large parts of most days with hours of unsupervised open-ended play; often, you couldn't.

There are a number of reasons why you couldn't. The two reasons that most social scientists agree have the greatest impact both come from the fact that your parents loved you so much - research shows they wanted to be parents more than any previous generation of parents.

They loved you so much that they wanted to provide you with every opportunity and so their tendencies were to fill your calendar with extracurricular activities - practices and lessons and scheduled activities packed on top of school nearly each day.

And their concern for your safety kept you and your friends from heading out unsupervised, exploring neighborhoods and parks and fields and woodlots to discover ways to fill the day.

Research shows your generation engaged in much less child's play compared to previous generations.

So, be generous with yourself - perhaps it takes an extra dose of humility - but do your creative mindset a great service and go enjoy some child's play.

Parents of young children:

Read the message to Millennials and please don't let that happen to your children.

Sure they have talents that should be cultivated. But they need to be bored, often, so they have to discover, and so they get to discover, just how creative they can be at amusing themselves.

Help them retain their creative genius by inviting lots of open-ended play.

ENTHUSIASTIC IN PURSUIT OF BEAUTY

This behavior first serves by refreshing you as you work at being and becoming creatively entrepreneurial.

You know how important it is to refresh your digital devices; their performance degrades when you don't and is quickly restored when you do.

Do you remember to refresh your most important device?

You? Your mind? Your body? Your mind and your body? Regularly? Frequently?

Enthusiastically pursuing beauty—intentionally watching for beauty— and then appreciating it deeply when you find it, is wonderfully refreshing.

It is interesting that across the most diverse cultural backgrounds we share so much in our understanding of what is beauty, but the effectiveness of this generative behavior doesn't rely on any common picture of beauty.

This behavior's restorative qualities work for you anytime you allow yourself to pay attention to what you think is beautiful long enough for you to relax, to take more than a deep breath, and to simply but fully behold that which you find beautiful.

Just be present to it. For more than a moment, and often.

"NOTHING
GREAT
WAS EVER
ACHIEVED
WITHOUT
ENTHUSIASM."

- RALPH WALDO EMERSON, AMERICAN
LITERARY ICON, 1803-1882

Being enthusiastic in your pursuit, in your discovery, and in your exploration of beauty compounds your reward, for beholding beauty also tunes and enriches your subconscious creative mindset.

It's true of all that is beautiful—natural or created—that the beauty is in the patterns and the relationships of color, of texture, of balance and form, or sound or movement.

So when you watch or listen generously and humbly—when you are open to beauty and perhaps even leaning into the experience—your creative mindset becomes more adept at finding patterns and discovering relationships that serve your generative work.

A 4 GENERATIVE BEHAVIORS KICKER

Each of the Generative Principles and strategies found in the matrix will serve you in lots of different ways, to accelerate the renewal and restoration of your creative genius by deploying the creative power of leveraging on your behalf.

Here's another, and it's fun to think about.

Research has determined that when you are in a bad mood, your peripheral vision narrows.

So it follows, does it not, that when you are in a good mood, your peripheral vision widens, to the maximum your physical characteristics allow.

I contend that if you are being generous and humble, playful and enthusiastic about the beauty in your life, you are very likely to be in the best mood the other circumstances of your life will allow.

So by intentionally practicing these 4 generative behaviors day in and day out your peripheral vision will tend to widen to its maximum range and you will see more of the world, so you get to see more patterns and more opportunity, and your subconscious will file it all away in your creative mindset for you, ready for when you need it.

And when you are working in a focused fashion on a creatively entrepreneurial initiative, then intentionally practicing the 4 generative behaviors should broaden your perspectives on the project and help you see aspects of it you might not have otherwise.

Creative exercise:

Earlier in the book I suggested you might want to keep a creative journal. It was a required assignment for my Duke students.

And one of the required categories of journal entries is for them to focus on each one of the 4 generative behaviors for a week and then write about or visualize what they felt or about how others reacted, and about what they learned.

You might want to give that a try, focusing intentionally on a generative behavior each week, as a Ready, Fire, Aim experiment. Just act on it and then consider what you learned.

STORY

The Generative Way Matrix reintroduces story to you as a technology.

I asked my students to consider language as the first open-sourced software—it's a fun exercise to stop for a moment and think about language as open-source software, and then consider the great advantage the English language has from being the most open-sourced language of all.

With language as the first open-source software, then story as a knowledge management technology was the first killer app.

Story as a knowledge management technology has been profoundly important to human development.

In fact, our use of story as a knowledge management technology shaped us as humans.

The technologies we used before we developed story have been labeled 'disposables' by anthropologists because our ancestors did so little to that stone, or to that stick, that it was more efficient to shape one in the moment it was needed than carry it around.

After language enabled story, our technologies transformed, and we had nets and baskets and designed more effective clothing and shelters because we learned that story:

- Could not only catalog and archive the instructions for creating and mastering making a net, for instance, and wow, that's a strong motivation to learn to use story....

- But story could also carry the contextual and motivational messages that would compel someone to try to make a net. That makes story both efficient and effectively creative.

Weaving a net when you've never done it before would be a fumbling, complicated and time consuming practice that would be easily avoided because of the power of the status quo if there wasn't a clear offer of advantage in the story of how to make one—string it across the stream and when you check it the next day, you have fish to eat.

- Then we discovered stories could honor our ancestors and keep them alive for us, and that gave us another reason to tell stories, to keep their wisdom present and in service of us.

- And then we discovered stories could entertain our clan, and that gave us another reason to tell each other stories.

- At some point we discovered aspirational stories, perhaps the most powerful use of story as technology. Aspirational stories told of a better way to live, about a finer human condition, and as we told them we found that telling them helped us live truer to our best aspirations.

Our stories have civilized us?

So for roughly 50,000 years we've all been telling each other all sorts of stories and listening to all sorts of stories. We've learned to understand our worlds through stories.

That's a significant strength of story as a knowledge management technology, that it is universal.

We all tell stories, we've all had our lives shaped by our favorite stories, we all understand who we are and hope to be through our stories.

We can rely on each other understanding each other through story.

Because of neuroplasticity—our brains' ability to grow new cognitive capacities as we use them for a particular purpose—the human brain became a highly refined storytelling machine a long time ago and each of us continues to nurture it as such, and we use it regularly, naturally, casually.

What can you do with your intentional use of this generative technology?

One of the most useful reasons to think of yourself as a storyteller when you are taking on a new project like a start-up or a new product is so you will remember to first think of prospective customers as your audience.

If you first treat them as an audience then they are more likely to become customers.

Before you sell anyone anything, before you tell anyone anything, you need to have their attention.

A storyteller knows there is no point in telling a story unless you have your audience's attention, and that the best way to attract that attention is to be attractive to them, and the best way to be attractive to an audience is to tell them THEIR story.

Nothing is more certain to capture your attention as an audience, and then hold it, than a story about you, about your hopes and your dreams and about how to make them happen.

I demonstrated this in a class of Duke undergrads by suggesting that if I had students in the classroom who wanted to attend NYU law school after graduation and I started telling a story I know about how a young lady not only got accepted to NYU but because she had worked so hard at developing her creatively entrepreneurial talents she arrived there with momentum, all tuned up and ready for a successful experience, and as I told the story if I got up and walked to the door and left the classroom and headed down the hall, telling the story, then every student who wanted to go to NYU will get up and follow me.

Your audience will work to be part of the story, to help the story come true, if it is a story about something significantly important to them, if it is their story.

When I tell you the story about something of significance to you and I make you a promise to deliver value that no one else is delivering to you, value that will enhance or appreciate what is significant to you, you will lean in hard, you will want to help me make that story come true.

Tell the audience their story and use your story as the promise to fulfill their dreams.

Story will do that for external audiences, and internal audiences.

Yes, internal audiences…employees.

Leaders should understand that story is such an insistent technology that if you share events or information with the folks in your organization and fail to provide them with a story that will help them make sense of it all, a story will be made up, by one or many, but soon there is a shared story that isn't yours.

The Generative Matrix considers story as a creative leadership technology.

I've never taken a business class of any sort, so the first time I had a job where I was going to manage a large business unit I went to a bookstore—this was the early to mid-80's—and purchased the business book it seemed everyone was buying then, *In Search of Excellence* by Peters and Waterman. Among the many great ideas the book organized so well, I was introduced to Management by Walking Around, MWA.

It seemed such an obvious idea to me then: that leaders can't sit in offices and expect to make good decisions, they have to be out and about, so they have the sense and feel for the business that the numbers can't capture, and so they are present and available to the folks getting the work done.

I found my natural tendency was to walk around telling stories. And the stories I would tell were about all the good stuff the folks around me were doing. I would catch people making decisions and taking actions that created advantage for us, or that served another, that improved our business, and then I would tell stories about that to others.

And as I practiced leadership by walking around telling these stories, I found more examples, and I kept telling stories about the performances that drove our success.

I did some of this almost every day.

The stories named names and described what they did and demonstrated why this served us so well.

Since our brains are story telling devices, since we want to think about all that is happening to us and all that is going on around us in narrative form, when you are working on a creative collaboration you will find that taking the work on as a story telling experience can get the whole team into their most effective creative mindsets and it serves as a useful template for creative exploration.

There's a three-part architecture to aspirational stories.

They are rooted in something demonstrably true today; they portray a better tomorrow; and they combine an offer with a promise—take this action, follow this route, and you can make it from here to that better tomorrow.

Selling a creative or entrepreneurial project to your boss or to investors or to your team can benefit from a story that doesn't just talk about the successes happening already but allows the energy of those emerging successes to carry the story forward, promising more to come.

The more people who believe in an aspirational story, the more likely it comes true.

Some aspirational stories simply need to be believed to start becoming realized.

Like the one about you being born to be a creative genius.

Creative exercise:

Write your six word creatively entrepreneurial autobiography.

On the website you will find a link to a great collection of six word autobiographies of a general nature.

Telling stories about you as a creatively entrepreneurial person helps you become a creatively entrepreneurial person.

IT'S SIMPLER THAN THEY TELL YOU.

- JOSH KRUGER

STRIVING TO REMAIN CHILDLIKE NOT -SH.

- MINGO REYNOLDS

THIS TIME, I ACTUALLY HIT SEND.

- NAOMI TSAI

Write your own six word creatively
entrepreneurial autobiography:

DIVERGENT DISCOVERY AND CONVERGENT CREATION

Linus Pauling's quote, about having lots of ideas, points us in the right direction but it stops short. If you want to have a really great idea you don't just need lots of ideas, you need lots of different types of ideas, so the solution you develop has the best chance of being the most effective.

That's where divergent discovery and convergent creation come into play.

These are two parts of one of the most fundamental and most frequently called upon creative cognitive process; it's a core idea generation and solution development process needed every time you find yourself in a ready fire aim discovery mode, so it's useful throughout the life of a creatively entrepreneurial project.

Because each part of this process operates very differently from the other, they are usually seen as two separate processes, one labeled divergent thinking and the other as convergent thinking—academic researchers always treat them separately and label them this way.

Because each part needs to work with the other seamlessly, TGWay matrix treats them as one process, and revises the names.

So divergent discovery is the more descriptive label for the front end of this combined process, because when trying to solve a problem or develop an opportunity you are discovering all the potential solutions and all the categories of solutions by exploring all the inputs and all the types of inputs you want to consider.

It's a diversity of options numbers game.

Considering lots of inputs over a diverse range is the goal of divergent discovery.

Have you already figured that divergent discovery is a useful tool to apply during your wondering while wandering? That using it helps your wandering become more effective, and brings broad purpose to your wondering.

Creative Exercise:

Based on your knowledge, and your imagination, what role do you think divergent discovery could have while you wonder and wander?

As I do the final edit of the first edition of this book I am just starting consulting with a start-up that is developing a new self-diagnostic medical device that will be launched at pharmacies. I will help them name the company and come up with positioning stories about who they serve and why that's important. I did start my divergent discovery with time on-line, learning more about the category generally, and reading what others are saying about it. But then over the next couple of days I became active, I became more creative by moving, and I visited a dozen pharmacies. I found good spots to hang out and just watch—who came, how long did they stay, did they show interest in signage—and then I talked to pharmacists about their view of the trends towards self-diagnostics, and when any of the customers there seemed approachable I asked them questions too.

I arrived not knowing what I was looking for except the right questions to ask.

After you have discovered a diverse collection of viable choices and plenty of unorthodox options, then you begin what others call convergent thinking but TGWay matrix calls convergent creation, playing with the inputs you've discovered, remixing them and mashing them and comparing and contrasting them, looking for patterns among them as you relate them again and again and again, taking interesting inputs from column A and two from column C and overlaying a sense of a new relationship you found in column D…and these inputs converge into your first thoughts for a solution that you'll test.

As my thinking on behalf of the medical device start-up develops and it is time to engage in convergent creation, and come up with the name and the story lines, I will return to wondering while wandering in the pharmacies as I ruminate on the various ideas, to create the most useful.

TGWay matrix offers divergent discovery and convergent creation as one process because in actual practice there isn't a clear break between discovery and creation; it's a series of overlapping cycles.

You aren't very far into your discovery of potential options and important inputs before you begin playing with first constructs, first new relationships, first fresh syntheses, and when an early convergence begins to look promising it will influence your continued divergent discovery as you test it, improve it, or discard it for now.

Soon enough, you are doing both, diverging and discovering while converging and creating, together, first one leads, then the other, building and testing, testing and refining, until you realize you've found the best solution, the smart way forward.

By the end of my first trips to pharmacies I was already 'testing' preliminary story directions.

Doing divergent discovery and convergent creation is a useful tool while wondering while wandering.

Another reason for the label revisions for this process is that divergent discovery and convergent creation adds alliteration, which aids memory.

And alliteration can add a touch of whimsy.

Always look for whimsy in your divergent discovery and convergent creation.

This dynamic process is not only key at the front end of your creative or entrepreneurial project—when you are wondering and wandering in the idea generation phase figuring out what you are going to do—it is useful every time you have important creative decisions to make during the execution phase as well.

You'll learn to scale your application of the process to the time allowed and the scope of the decision, but this generative tool is useful throughout your creatively entrepreneurial work.

As with other concepts organized in TGWay matrix, when you

intentionally get used to this it becomes part of your creative mindset and begins serving you without you being aware.

Divergent discovery and convergent creation benefit from you intentionally being the creative deviant.

You want perspectives no one else has taken so you can see opportunity no one else has seen.

Being a contrarian is one way to be the creative deviant.

Start by being a contrarian with your own previously held views or beliefs.

Being playful is another way to be a creative deviant.

Being humble is another.

Kaleidoscopic Thinking is a useful visual prompt for how convergent creation works.

I'll bet you have a good sense of how something labeled kaleidoscopic thinking would serve you during divergent discovery and convergent creation even before I share the quote from Rosabeth Moss Kanter:

CREATIVITY IS A LOT LIKE
LOOKING AT THE WORLD
THROUGH A KALEIDOSCOPE.
YOU LOOK AT A SET OF
ELEMENTS, THE SAME ONES
EVERYONE ELSE SEES, BUT
THEN REASSEMBLE THOSE
FLOATING BITS AND PIECES INTO
AN ENTICING NEW POSSIBILITY.
EFFECTIVE LEADERS ARE ABLE
TO SHAKE UP THEIR THINKING
AS THOUGH THEIR BRAINS ARE
KALEIDOSCOPES, PERMITTING AN
ARRAY OF DIFFERENT PATTERNS
OUT OF THE SAME BITS OF
REALITY.

- ROSABETH MOSS KANTER

The inputs and ideas you discover are important, but it is often the relationships between them where opportunity is found. So keep playing with those relationships.

There are divergent discovery and convergent creation exercises on the website. You'll also find research proving that your natural capacities to engage in divergent discovery and convergent creation will improve when you practice them.

BOTH

When discovering the solution to a problem or weighing our options we often think the answer is 'either/or'.

As divergent discovery and convergent creation show, the creative insight or opportunity is often found in a new relationship between things.

I learned a whole new way to consider relationships, through the power of both, at the side of a creek.

It was a Sunday morning, I was driving home down a quiet country road, low swampy woods on both sides. Up ahead, crossing the road, it was hard to tell at first, but yes, it was two shapes, very small critters of some sort, in a jerky locomotion and not making much progress fast, so I pulled my pick-up over and discovered they were two baby snapping turtles, likely hatched in the previous 48 hours.

When I picked up these perfect miniatures of the 40 pound adults they become in about 10 years--they can live most of a century, and some specimens get as big as 80 pounds--one of them disappeared into its shell and the other stuck its neck out as far as it would go, and opened its mouth to threaten me.

To give them a better chance to reach 100 years I decided to put them in my truck to drive the mile or so to the path I knew that would lead deep into the woods to a creek, and I would release them there.

So I did, and I placed the two baby snapping turtles in the creek water, and in the blink of an eye, they were gone; they had each vanished in an instant, but by following very different strategies--one disappeared into the soft mud creek bottom, and the other darted into the deepest water.

And so whatever predator was after them, one of them would have survived.

I was staggered by the beauty of it—it made me weak in the knees while my spirit soared. I found myself on my knees, humbled by nature's balance and grace.

I was walking back through the woods when the creative lesson came to me. I saw that opposites can be reconciled when the right question is asked. In this case it wasn't a question about how a baby snapping turtle should behave when threatened; it was a question about how a sufficient number from the clutch of baby snapping turtles survives over time for that reproductive cycle to have been successful.

And I thought about how often I have been challenged, when doing creative work, to bring together disparate thoughts or ideas or actions and felt like I had to choose one over the other, or compromise the two which usually results in something less than the outcome I was working towards.

I now saw that when faced with interesting or attractive opposite ideas or solutions, I should step back and reconsider the question I am trying to answer, or the strategy I am trying to develop, and see if I can reformulate it, restate it, so that both can be true.

It was years later that someone helped me understand the immediate effect watching these snapping turtles had on me—I felt I was present to something sacred—when he defined transcendence as the reconciliation of two opposites.

You transcend previous limitations and something new is created.

And that's what we are trying to do so often in the creative process; we are trying to find that relationship between two things previously unrelated.

We are attempting a transcendence.

It comes from asking better questions.

SERVANT LEADERSHIP

I didn't study servant leadership, not at first.

First, I got used to it, from the back of a boat, as a fishing guide, at Barney's Ball Lake Lodge on the English River in northwestern Ontario.

The men who came to the fishing camp were successful—presidents of corporations, partners in their law firms or ad agencies, sportscasters and actors— and some of better known included James Hoffa, Natalie Wood, the Getty Oil Brothers, and John Wayne.

The first summer I guided these men — I didn't have the good fortune to guide Ms. Wood — was the summer I turned 16.

It didn't take me long to figure out that, like the rest of us, these men (there in the mid to late 1960's, it was almost always men) liked to be served and so that's what I did, to the best of my talents and abilities.

I asked what time they wanted to be awakened for the day of fishing the river and woke them at their cabins with a fresh pot of coffee and any breakfast treat I could steal from the kitchen.

When they were at breakfast I carried their tackle from their cabin to the boat.

I asked about their drink preferences, and made sure our ice bucket was well stocked with what they wanted.

And I checked their tackle boxes with them before we left the first day to make sure they were outfitted properly and I provided the clearest description I could of what conditions each fishing spot provided.

I found that as I served them better their response was to grant me more authority over them; I used that authority to serve them better still— for instance I began to narrate their day for them, helping them fully appreciate the significance of what they were doing, as I was getting used to the power of story—and soon I was fully vested with all the authority I needed to lead them through the day.

I started as *a* guide and soon became *their* guide and often they wanted me to be the captain.

When as an entrepreneur I was in leadership roles, recruiting talent and helping folks get their best work accomplished, I did study servant leadership.

What I read affirmed my natural instincts (yes, I do think I am part of the 98% of us who were born creative geniuses) that the best way to make sure you attract the best people to join your company and do their best work is to let them know that you are going to keep recruiting them, even after they have agreed to join up, you are going to keep recruiting them, every day you are going to work hard to help them enjoy doing their best work and you are going to help them find new challenges and you are going to help them grow their skills and abilities.

When I made that sort of promise to talented folks and then consistently acted on it they would grant me all the authority I needed to do my job most effectively and I got to enjoy the generative lift—of my company's performance and my sense of well-being—that comes of executing the servant leadership strategy.

It seemed like a very easy pre-emptive creative solution to all sorts of management issues—all I had to do was deliver on a promise to help people do their best work, and incredible creative work was accomplished, regularly.

Servant leadership is a great way to find friends fast while you are wandering and wondering. When you serve the people you meet, you generate a social network loaded with creatively entrepreneurial energy.

It's another example of that pragmatic altruism that is so generative.

And the reciprocity that generosity tends to generate helps turn your social capital into creative capital—when you are taking care for others they tend to want to take care for you.

Another picture of the sort of humility The Generative Way offers: that you place the people who report to you above you—that you would see your job as being their servant.

The best authority to have, the only authority that is meaningful and creatively useful, is that which is granted to you.

A GENERATIVE WAY STORY

A Story to illuminate some TGWay matrix concepts—with special attention given to the effectiveness of the dynamics of Ready Fire Aim discovery.

It's been my goal throughout this book to provide you with many perspectives on these concepts, so you can make them your own. Here's one of my favorite perspectives.

The story is about Mark Bowles and the founding of ecoATM. Mark is a very successful and very creative entrepreneur, and my friend and brother-in-law.

ecoATM is the world's first fully-automated eWaste recycling center. Their intelligent, self-serve, free standing kiosks—located in high foot-traffic areas in malls for example—appraise your mobile handsets, MP3 players, and tablets and pay cash on the spot for those they can resell and they will responsibly recycle those they can't.

Mark has been a founder, a co-founder, and board level founder's advisor of nearly a dozen start-ups. After 17 years and 5 start-ups in Silicon Valley, Mark is now very active in the San Diego venture incubator scene, and invests a lot of time mentoring entrepreneurs and students who are starting new businesses.

Before ecoATM, Mark had no experience in the kiosk or recycling industries but was familiar with the mobile handset space through his work on wireless chipsets and microprocessors that targeted that market. In fact his experience with this space began before his start-up days, when he worked in Silicon Valley for Motorola Semiconductors, back in the late 80's and early 90's.

Mark, now living in La Jolla, Ca, is one of the folks I think of immediately when I consider the practical value of wondering while wandering.

Mark's wandering is energetic. He is constantly playing with new ideas and exploring new places—he took up surfing in his 40's and his most recent start-up idea—post-ecoATM—takes him into another new direction, the life sciences world.

And his wondering is constant. He is always questioning, inviting other to wonder along with him about something that's caught his fancy.

He is often the respectful contrarian, asking challenging questions but always with an appreciative eye to creating advantage for all involved.

After his start-up previous to ecoATM fell short, Mark started his energetic wondering and wandering to discover what to do next. He didn't restrict himself to the comfort of the technology areas he was most familiar with already. Instead, he considered a broad spectrum of potential problems to solve regardless of the technology required.

Early on he made two discoveries that brought initial focus to his wondering and his wandering.

He found industry research that estimated that the typical American household had 5 to 7 retired mobile handsets, lying about in a drawer or a box somewhere, most of them operational and in good shape, kept because there was a general sense that they were a toxic danger if thrown away with the household trash. He learned that only 3% of people worldwide reported that they had ever recycled one of their mobile phones and the year of that study, 2008, there were nearly 1B mobile phones shipped.

And Mark found a large and growing demand for used mobile handsets that wasn't being met.

There was great demand overseas, in developing nations, where local distribution was in place to get product into the communities but were starved for product to sell.

As his exploration continued, Mark found other markets for used handsets, including the refurbish and repair and insurance markets.

So that framed a key early challenge that would shape so much of his first discovery: how to effectively and efficiently collect the retired handsets so he could deliver them to these markets.

The retired handsets were out of sight, and mostly out of mind, and considered to be of no value since brand new mobile handsets are so cheap. And if folks thought of them at all is was as a minor irritation since the toxic materials complicated their disposal; most folks were happy to keep them out of sight and out of mind.

It's really hard and expensive work to get a consumer to think differently about something, and Mark's challenge was that folks really didn't want to think about their used handsets at all.

Mark quickly discovered he was not the first to be looking at this opportunity.

He found a small handful of players, each trying to solve that big collection challenge with their own riffs on the same collection strategy: using paid media, often late night cable, their offer was that if you mail us your phones then we'll appraise them and send you cash if they have value.

Mark saw a couple of what he considered to be fatal flaws with this collection strategy.

Creative Exercise:

What flaws do you see in what could be called the 'cash for gold' collection strategy?

No matter how effective the message, paid media just didn't seem sustainable to him.

And to promise you might get cash later, after you do all the work, seemed to be no promise at all. Mark knew in his gut that instant cash would be a powerful offer; this idea was conceived and launched in the early days of the 2008 Great Recession.

Early on Mark realized that one of the biggest challenges that would emerge for a successful company in this space was how it would handle the huge number of electronic devices that had no commercial value— eWaste—and it would be his company's job to recycle them. One of the leading companies in the business at the time was founded by a man who was also serious about the environmental challenge, and seemed to be holding his company to the highest standards of environmental responsibility, so in the spirit of finding friends fast, Mark reached out to him.

Mark told him of his intent to start a company that would pioneer an improved collection strategy—acknowledging they would be competitors if he did—and he shared his appreciation for their recycling program. He suggested that even if they were competitors, it might make sense for them to work at the recycling challenge together, and Mark visited their operations. He made a new friend, two men who were determined to grow this category and who took seriously the environmental challenge and who were open to the possibility they may work together.

Along the way and throughout, Mark was getting reacquainted with old friends, both folks he knew from his mobile handset industry days, and also venture capitalists.

Mark is an expert at cultivating the key influencers of success early on in the project—the venture capitalists and other investors if your idea will need financial capital, or your boss or client or anyone you will need to like your idea. As Mark's ideas for this company were just taking shape—he called it reMobile at first—he began to talk about it with VC's, asking for their ideas and advice about what a successful company in this space would look like, with no mention of investment.

Mark does this authentically, selecting folks he respects and listening generously to their thoughts and ideas. So when he later pitches the version of the idea ready for investing or approving, those on the other side of the table have participated in the building of the idea, and even if they maintain their place on the other side of the table they are also participants in the story.

Before Mark discovered the intelligent freestanding kiosk idea, he considered a range of other collection strategies. One that we worked on together was the Boy Scouts; that they could organize collection drives as one of their major fund raising projects. But that would be short lived each year, no more than a month or so, so with them as a model, we tried to identify other organizations so that every month, someone somewhere would be collecting phones.

We soon abandoned it as too clunky, way too unwieldy; even if we got it to work effectively it was riddled with inefficiencies.

Other collection strategies considered in those earliest days included a simple drop-off type kiosk (used devices would be collected but instead of instant cash, devices would be evaluated later and a check would be sent to the user), and school and club fund-raisers using charity boxes.

It was Mark's actual wandering in the real physical world that paid off in the most valuable fashion for the founding of the company.

He'd been building his creative capital, considering and talking and wondering all over the category terrain, making deep impressions on his subconscious, so his creative mindset was prepped for the day he was walking from his car to a Starbucks to meet again with some founding friends to talk about this opportunity.

It was the fifth or sixth time they'd met there; by then they had been focusing on discovering a technology solution for the collection challenge. As Mark walked past the CoinStar kiosk that sat outside the Starbucks—CoinStar is the intelligent free-standing kiosk that converts loose change to dollars or store coupons—this time the kiosk's presence fully registered with him. And once it did the idea for the best collection strategy for mobile handsets came to him, if not fully formed, certainly fully framed.

And of course it wasn't fully formed. The kiosk would need to make a real time evaluation and appraisal of the multiple qualities of the phone that made up its resale value—from its make and model to its operating condition to its physical appearance to the current resale market's appetite—and that was a complex technology deployment. Developing those technologies was its own process of divergent discovery and convergent creation, and of filling each inch and every minute with their most creatively entrepreneurial efforts, and Mark came out of it with 40 plus patents and patent applications in his name for this technology.

But the intelligent free standing kiosk strategy did come to Mark fully framed, and he knew immediately this technology solution would break through against the next big challenge they would face—getting folks to think and do something new with their retired handsets when they don't want to think about them at all.

He could see that when he placed an intelligent freestanding kiosk in a high foot traffic area with the proper messaging that conveyed immediate cash payouts for resalable used mobile handsets and responsible recycling for the others, and folks walked past the message day after day, they would finally get the message, just as he finally realized the CoinStar's presence.

Then it was a small change in human behavior—folks simply needed to remember to grab their old phones on the next trip to the mall.

So Mark was ready to test and learn and test and learn; to fail fast and fail often and fail cheap.

First off he was determined to test the underlying premise of the kiosk concept itself. So the founding friends got together and designed and built a shell of the idea, a dumb plywood kiosk—no technology at all but messages and graphics to make it appear operational—and they loaded it into a pick-up and drove from Southern California to Omaha Nebraska where one of the country's largest discount retailers (owned by Warren Buffet) would allow them to place the kiosk in a very high foot-traffic area.

They would generate a tremendous number of very real interactions.

Once the kiosk was in place Mark and his founding friends—Eric Rosser, Bob Genthert, Tom Tullie, Vincent Dorian, and others——decided they would stand back and blend into the crowd and wait until someone stopped, read the messages, and then acted as if they wanted to make the kiosk work. At that point they would step forward and lead the individual through the transaction, engaging and listening—they weren't studying their opportunity, they were getting used to it.

The growth in passerby interest from day to day was remarkable, better than they hoped it would be. Here's how Mark summarizes the extraordinary results of this test:

> "On the first day we collected 23 phones. Over the next couple of days we collected a growing number but by the fourth day we had a constant waiting line 8 to 10 people deep eager to sell us their used devices. And it was all word-of-mouth or by simply stumbling upon the kiosk in the store. We were having to empty the kiosk twice a day because it would become jammed and overflow with phones. By the end of this initial 30 day trial we had collected over 2300 used devices, exceeded our revenue goal by over 1000%, had attracted the attention of the local and national press, and had learned a tremendous amount about our customers and market by interacting with nearly 750 customers face to face. And our host, Nebraska Furniture Mart, was

begging us to keep the kiosk there. In 30 days we had taken all of the theory, challenged it, validated most of it, and learned with specificity how and why consumers and retailers preferred our specific solution. As was our initial goal for this project, we validated the solution in the market that was capable of inspiring mass consumer participation in eWaste recycling by providing immediate incentive and convenience. The main assumptions we had arrived at through our wondering and wandering were validated and expanded."

The next few years for Mark and ecoATM were about converting this initial trial success into investor funding (eventually nearly $40M in venture investment and another $40M in mezzanine debt), deep R&D on fully-automating the kiosk with machine vision, artificial intelligence, and electrical inspection (resulting in 45 patents and patent applications), building a world-class team of over 200 direct and indirect employees, launching nearly 1000 kiosks into 42 states, collecting several million devices, and paying out 10's of millions of dollars to consumers, and eventually selling the company to Outerwall (aka Coinstar) for $350M.

CLOSING THOUGHTS

Some closing thoughts and a lasting challenge.

I practice Ready Fire Aim in all of my creative and entrepreneurial work, including my writing. When I started writing my first novel, The 53rd Parallel, I had no idea I was starting a trilogy of novels based on my time as a fishing guide in Ontario; I had a vague idea of the stories I wanted to tell as I just started writing.

And I was surprised every day by what came next in the stories I was telling.

And I was constantly re-writing, which continually improved my work.

When I started writing this book, I knew it was an introduction of The Generative Way but had no idea what the conclusion would be, nor did I know I would tease you about sustainable abundance throughout. Once I began playing with sustainable abundance I got the sense that this intriguing concept would be the conclusion.

And then I had a second idea for the conclusion, that I would urge you and maybe coach you on organizing and designing your own creatively entrepreneurial matrix from the concepts you already relied upon and any new ones you have made your own from TGWay matrix I have offered here.

Designing your matrix would create a dynamic tool to apply when you are focused on a creative challenges and designing it will imprint the creative concepts and entrepreneurial strategies deeper into your subconscious, making it more likely you perform as your best creatively entrepreneurial self in the inches and the minutes of your daily life.

Some tips on building your own matrix:

How will you be applying your creatively entrepreneurial genius in the future, to what purpose? Perhaps you could design your matrix with that in mind.

For the past few years my application of creatively entrepreneurial concepts has been primarily as a teacher, so I designed TGWay matrix as an education tool first and foremost; I was of course delighted that I am personally served by it as well.

Be visual. When you can capture your thoughts and ideas visually you are very likely to understand them better. Plus, it's fun. And draw it really big, someplace, and I mean really big.

Revise it continually. Your regular revision is a regular refreshment of how you are thinking, perceiving, and behaving as a creatively entrepreneurial person.

Finally, what do I mean by *sustainable abundance*?

What have you come up with?

Start with standard dictionary definitions of each word—for sustainable we find definitions like 'able to be maintained at a certain rate or level' and 'harvesting a resource without depleting it' and for abundance we get 'a very large quantity of something'. (Note it's very large, not just large.)

Hmmm…creating very large quantities that can be harvested without depleting.

That sure seems to be a worthwhile goal for organizing a creatively entrepreneurial matrix, and a life: creating plenty for everyone, from now on.

Can that be taken seriously? It sure sounds utopian when considered on a large scale. But what if I try to apply it to the scale I operate on daily, my local world.

It seems that striving for a sustainable abundance would include:

Well, it needs a very large dose of this core human quality of being and becoming creatively entrepreneurial, a quality that doesn't get depleted but grows and grows with its application.

And if being generous begets others being generous, then let's keep being generous with each other.

And when approaching an opportunity or a resource sustainable abundance suggests I shouldn't 'take advantage' of it, but rather I should 'create advantage' from it.

How about aspirational stories—they are sustainable and call forth more than what currently exists.

And I like servant leadership as the climate control operating mode that will nurture the best of others and make it much more likely they grow as they offer their best.

Thanks for reading this book; please share it with your friends and I want to remind you that there is more on the website.

And my parting hope for all of you is that you find ways to apply your growing creative genius to discovering and creating a sustainable abundance in your work and play.

ABOUT THE AUTHOR

Carl Nordgren has spent a lifetime writing this book.

He first worked for a start-up in 1979 and has founded a half dozen companies since as well as assisted in the founding of a dozen more; he's worked in four of the creative industries; he's published three novels including the award winning *Anung's Journey* and the International Best Seller *The 53rd Parallel*; from 2002 to 2016 he was adjunct faculty at Duke and taught over 3,500 undergrads how to be the most creative and entrepreneurial versions of themselves they could be.

His first job was a fishing guide, from the summer of 1966 to the summer of 1970; if he wasn't in high school or college he was guiding on the English River in wilderness Ontario and the White River in the Ozarks of Arkansas, where he learned a lot about bringing creative thinking and entrepreneurial behavior to the inches and the minutes of each day.

He credits his wife Marie as a powerful influence on his work, through her nurturing of creative genius in their children and in her preschool nursery based on the Waldorf child development principles.

They have three daughters, Krista Anne, Brita, and Sarah Rose, and he and Marie enjoy watching them flourish.

ABOUT THE DESIGNER

Kevin Qian met Carl as a student at Duke University.

Under Carl's mentorship, Kevin's initial desire to pursue a future in finance evolved into a revived interest in creative arts. He now thrives in the commercial design world only several years after graduation. He currently guides creative direction at a digital marketing firm and is also the owner of Q Branding, a boutique design company based in Detroit, MI where he currently resides.

MORE

For more information about becoming a creative genius, {again}, visit:

creativepopulist.com

Also by Carl Nordgren:

The 53rd Parallel

Worlds Between

Anung's Journey

For more information about Nordgren's novels visit:

carlnordgren.com

CPSIA information can be obtained
at www.ICGtesting.com
Printed in the USA
FFHW012105160119
50126927-55012FF

9 781611 532166